SUMMARY

OF

WOMEN ROWING NORTH

BY MARY PIPHER

NAVIGATING LIFE'S CURRENTS AND FLOURISHING AS WE AGE

BY

BookNation Publishing

COPYRIGHT

DISCLAIMER

TABLE OF CONTENTS

• As we advance in age, we have to deal with many new difficulties on top of old, familiar ones. So for us to be happy at this stage of life, we have to change our thinking and our behavior. We must change our attitudes and acquire the new set of skills we

•   So as we age, crises will come. Our identities will reform. We will engage with transformations in various aspects of our lives.

But in all, to survive and thrive as older women we must reconstruct new meanings for ourselves and repurpose our lives. 25

- We can achieve this through the choices we make (what, when, where, and how we choose). Remember that we older folks have that power of choice and that our choice is the key that can open up reserves of dignity and well-being for us. 25

- If we must thrive as we age, we must learn new skills and acquire new habits. What worked in times past, and what we used to do easily in the days of yore may no longer be easily possible or possible at all...25

- Thus we need new understandings, new frameworks, new and better navigational know-hows and capabilities to be able to survive and thrive in this stage. 26

- What we must do is to develop a new perspective and attitude towards life. We must begin to see all of our experiences, all of our pains, joys and challenges at this stage as beautiful gifts, each presenting us with an opportunity to learn and grow..................26

- Thus we must welcome every experience (negative of positive). We must understand and welcome our fading or faded beauty, our physically weakened and restricted bodies, and our loss of social position, power and control. Basically we must construct these new experiences as valuable crucibles of knowledge from which we can learn new skills and capabilities. .26

- We also need to be resilient to survive and thrive at this stage. And resilience is not fixed. You can pick it up. You can learn it just as you can learn to cook a Chinese dish or learn a new board game...26

- We also need to keep growing in order to survive and thrive at this stage. But growth is evitable. So we must choose to grow and to invest the necessary effort required to do so. We can still make this choice right now because it is simply never too late to choose to grow.

• We older women must craft for ourselves a space and place in this society with our own new goals and responsibilities. We can each learn to be arbiters of our society's moral imagination. We can also learn to be exemplary survivors amidst the roughest of currents. And we can also learn to be society's paragons of courage.

• Old age comes with its joys and sufferings. All life stages do. But attitude and intentionality are the lords of this stage. With the right attitude, aging can be redeeming and compensatory. But we must embrace both the suffering and the joys that come with this life stage, so that we can grow from them.

• Even as old folks we can put ourselves in a desirable place via the power in our choices, our intentionality, our resilience, our attitude and plain old gratitude. These can enable us to navigate and adapt in this life stage.

• We must not fear loss or suffering. There is, after all, recovery after loss. Most women who lose their life partners still recover and push ahead. Besides, suffering can also be advantageous and beneficial, and perhaps, even important and necessary in more ways than one.

• Well-being may well reside on the obverse of catastrophe. That is the duality in our condition. And we must meet this understanding with the contentment and wisdom that come with this life stage.

• You must note this. In fact, write it down somewhere and read it to yourself everyday: *"We can joyfully and successfully navigate, survive and thrive as we journey down the path of time. It can be fun. It must be fun. We shall make it fun!"*

INTRODUCTION

KEY TAKEAWAYS

- I am now approaching seventy years of age and I have written this book about us older women and the peculiar issues we face as we transit from middle age to "elderhood" (aka old age). This book therefore deals with how older women can develop those strong mechanisms that we need to cope with the peculiar difficulties that come with this stage of life. How do we navigate around life's difficulties at old age? How do we cope as we age? This book answers these questions, and more.

- At every new phase of life, we find that the coping mechanisms that used to work for us in the past are not nearly as useful anymore in the present. In this stage of our lives we must learn new coping mechanisms. This book fills that need

- As we get older, control gradually recedes from us. But we do have one very important thing, and that thing is "choice". We have the choice to accept or decline. We have the choice to permit or deny. We have the choice to participate or to avoid. Our choice is our power. And it can help us to transit resiliently into wholly-adjusted and fulfilled adults.

- We can become ever more joyful and happier as we advance in age. And ideally we should become nicer and kinder to ourselves.

- As we advance in age, we have to deal with many new difficulties on top of old, familiar ones. So for us to be happy at this stage of life, we have to change our thinking and our behavior. We must change our attitudes and acquire the new set of skills we need to cope. We must jettison the past, welcome the change, and adapt, so we can move forward.

- In old age, we tend to lose parts of our identity. But not to worry because we nevertheless add even newer parts, and expand on several aspects of our identity. We are able to improvise and assume new and more important roles.

- Not every older woman grows into becoming an elder. This is because growth does not happen by itself. Growth requires effort from us. It requires us to put in the effort required to acquire new skills necessary for us to transit successfully and gracefully into "elderhood".

- We should learn to embrace all that life throws at us and savor each experience, good or bad. Those are what life is made of. And each experience bears a gift that we must recognize and exploit to our benefit. In old age, regardless of our situation, we can still (we must still) find our joy, our inner peace and wisdom.

- As we travel along the rivers of time we must be deliberate and kind to ourselves in our choices. We must carry a positive attitude, and maintain a strong sense of purpose, always. And remember that there is still a lot of life to live and live it to the max!

SUMMARY

I am now approaching seventy years of age and I feel that women my age (and some in their sixties) are at a cross road. We are at a border in life where many interesting and significant things happen and a lot of changes occur. So my focus in this book is on older women who, much like me, are perched on this precipice of change that invariably requires us to expand our identities. Therefore, Women Rowing North deals with the peculiar issues women face as we transit from middle age to "elderhood" (aka old age).

At this phase of life, our central preoccupation is figuring out how we can develop the strong mechanisms we need to cope with those peculiar difficulties that come at this stage. How do we navigate around life's difficulties at old age? How do we cope as we age?

At every new phase of life, we find that the coping mechanisms that used to work for us in the past are not nearly as useful anymore in the present. We therefore find ourselves in a situation where we are faced with a greater number of difficulties than we can manage or had been prepared to handle. If we end up unable to cope with this stage of life, if we end up not grow bigger enough to handle the new set of problems, we may become embittered.

Attitude or frame of mind isn't all there is to everything. It isn't the only thing that matters, however it is nearly all there is to everything. Truth be told, in the many situations we will face as we age, attitude is all we have. It is all we can have.

The truth is that as we get older, it becomes obvious that we do not and cannot have control over most things at all times or at least as much as we would love to. Control gradually recedes from us. But we do have one very important thing, and that thing is "choice".

We are older people, and we have the power of choice. We have the choice to accept or decline. We have the choice to permit or deny. We have the choice to participate or to avoid. We have that capacity. Indeed it's a right we reserve. This choice that we have is power. And it can determine whether we become dormant and decline into reactivity and pessimism or whether we continue to move forward, to grow resiliently into wholly-adjusted and fulfilled adults.

It is true that pain, distress, sorrow and outrage will expectedly remain with us as humans, but with will, deliberateness, the right skills, and a good attitude, we can become ever more joyful and happier as we advance in age.

As we advance in age, we have to deal with ageism and peculiar gender–based difficulties. Also as we age, our brains, and physical bodies and our sexuality are depreciated and discounted. Furthermore, many negative generalizations and stereotypes about older women abound. For instance mother-in-law jokes are all about us older women and suggest that we are intrusive, obtrusive, domineering, opinionated, and unwelcome troublemakers.

For us to be happy at his stage of life, we can't simply accept being a reduced rendition of our previously youthful selves. No, that is not it. Instead, to be happy, we should change our thinking and our behavior. We must change our attitudes and acquire the new set of skills we need to cope. We must jettison the past (it ain't coming back no more, so move on), welcome the change, and adapt, so we can experience the insight, realness and bliss that is possible and abundant at this stage of life.

In old age, we tend to lose parts of our identity. But we nevertheless add even newer parts to our identity and expand on several aspects of it. We also tend to lose some long-held roles, yet we are able to improvise new, and perhaps, more important ones. And ideally we should become nicer and kinder to ourselves.

This book, *Women Rowing North* initiates a fresh dialogue about the intricacy, difficulties, talents and gifts of older women. Despite that our culture depicts older women as unhappy, regretful, and mean, the fact remains, however, that we are mostly profoundly happy. Indeed, the majority of women experience greater happiness beginning from around fifty five years of age, with their level of happiness increasing as they get even older. My argument in this book is that our happiness is not as a result of genetics or environment but depends on how we have learnt to handle whatever life throws our way.

Not every older woman grows into becoming an elder. This is because growth does not happen by itself. Growth requires effort from us, It requires us to put in the effort required to acquire new skills necessary for attuning our perspectives, managing our internal dialogues, managing our emotions, creating joy within us, and nurturing healthy relationships. Building such skills imbue us with the emotional resilience.

Old age can be arduous. Older people experience loss more frequently (of family members, friends, colleagues and those we love). In old age, doctor's offices and funerals become ever more familiar to us. But we must be able to navigate through this phase successfully. It demands flexibility, tolerance, openness, and the ability to run all our experiences through a "positive" filter before we absorb them. In other words, old age requires certain navigational skills, but the good news is that it is our old age (our long history and experience) that also grants us the wherewithal to acquire those navigational skills that we need.

If we acquire these navigational skills, we will experience the type of growth that prepares us for successful aging. We should learn to embrace all that life throws at us. Savor each experience, good or bad. And note that those are the fabric of life. Those are what life is made of. And each experience bears a gift that we must recognize and exploit to our benefit. In old age, and regardless of whatever we may have been through or may be going through, we can still (we must still) find our joy, our inner peace and wisdom.

Women Rowing North is the guidebook that carries this golden message. Indeed everything (yes, everything!) is possible and beautiful because it is all life, all life's stuff. And life is beautiful. Women Rowing North prescribes that we develop our mental "positive" filter and that thereafter we will witness that everything (yes, everything!), works for our good. There is always an answer, always a way out, always a solution, always a helping hand, always happiness, always joy. Joy abounds. Joy is infinite. It always eventually works out!

As we travel along the rivers of time toward the land of winter, snow and ice, we need to stay on course. To do so requires effort. We must put effort into gracefully and successfully passing through this phase. We must be deliberate and kind to ourselves in our choices. We must carry a positive attitude, and maintain a strong sense of purpose, always. And remember that there is still a lot of life to live. Yes, with the right attitude, so much can be packed into every minute, every experience that each one feels like a life time! There is still a lot of life to live at this phase.

Live it like the champion you are!

Live it to the max!

CHAPTER 1: A NEW STRETCH OF THE RIVER

KEY TAKEAWAYS

- Only one thing is truly constant in this universe and that thing is change. Life itself is founded on change, hence life is unpredictable. And change brings crises. But such is life!

- So as we age, crises will come. Our identities will reform. We will engage with transformations in various aspects of our lives. But in all, to survive and thrive as older women we must reconstruct new meanings for ourselves and repurpose our lives.

- We can achieve this through the choices we make (what, when, where, and how we choose). Remember that we older folks have that power of choice and that our choice is the key that can open up reserves of dignity and well-being for us.

- If we must thrive as we age, we must learn new skills and acquire new habits. What worked in times past, and what we used to do easily in the days of yore may no longer be easily possible or possible at all.

- Thus we need new understandings, new frameworks, new and better navigational know-hows and capabilities to be able to survive and thrive in this stage.

- What we must do is to develop a new perspective and attitude towards life. We must begin to see all of our experiences, all of our pains, joys and challenges at this stage as beautiful gifts, each presenting us with an opportunity to learn and grow.

- Thus we must welcome every experience (negative of positive). We must understand and welcome our fading or faded beauty, our physically weakened and restricted bodies, and our loss of social position, power and control. Basically we must construct these new experiences as valuable crucibles of knowledge from which we can learn new skills and capabilities.

- We also need to be resilient to survive and thrive at this stage. And resilience is not fixed. You can pick it up. You can learn it just as you can learn to cook a Chinese dish or learn a new board game.

- We also need to keep growing in order to survive and thrive at this stage. But growth is evitable. So we must choose to grow and to invest the necessary effort required to do so. We can still make this choice right now because it is simply never too late to choose to grow.

- We older women must craft for ourselves a space and place in this society with our own new goals and responsibilities. We can each learn to be arbiters of our society's moral imagination. We can also learn to be exemplary survivors amidst the roughest of currents. And we can also learn to be society's paragons of courage.

- Old age comes with its joys and sufferings. All life stages do. But attitude and intentionality are the lords of this stage. With the right attitude, aging can be redeeming and compensatory. But we must embrace both the suffering and the joys that come with this life stage, so that we can grow from them.

- Even as old folks we can put ourselves in a desirable place via the power in our choices, our intentionality, our resilience, our attitude and plain old gratitude. These can enable us to navigate and adapt in this life stage.

- We must not fear loss or suffering. There is, after all, recovery after loss. Most women who lose their life partners still recover and push ahead. Besides, suffering can also be advantageous and beneficial, and perhaps, even important and necessary in more ways than one.

- Well-being may well reside on the obverse of catastrophe. That is the duality in our condition. And we must meet this understanding with the contentment and wisdom that come with this life stage.

- You must note this. In fact, write it down somewhere and read it to yourself everyday: ***"We can joyfully and successfully navigate, survive and thrive as we journey down the path of time. It can be fun. It must be fun. We shall make it fun!"***

SUMMARY

There is no single lifetime. Well, what I mean is that any given lifetime contains several other lifetimes within it. I know this because I have experienced these several lifetimes myself within my life (time). I am or have been a student, a mother, a wife, a grandmother, a musician, a psychologist, a therapist, and a writer/speaker. These are all lifetimes.

There have been connections and cohesion between these lifetimes. For example, regardless of whatever lifetime I am experiencing, I must keep on reading books, because I have always loved to read. I have also always loved the outdoors, swimming, long walks, and just gazing at the sky. I have also always loved, and taken care of my family, best friends and people and animals, generally. These have all been the constants, continuities that have held me in place through my several lifetimes.

But there have also been some unconnectedness, some discontinuities between these lifetimes. For example I can barely recognize the pre-teen version of me. I can also find little connection to the recently-graduated version of me. These earlier versions of me seem, now, not to be connected to who and what I am today.

Growing up and going through these various lifetimes sometimes feels like emerging into a different time capsule each time with a realization of my personal vulnerability (another continuity). Yet I am aware that only one thing is truly constant in this universe and that thing is change. In fact, life itself is founded on change, hence life is unpredictable. Change brings crises. It brings conflict, unease, pain and suffering but that is just how it is. That is just the fundamental nature of life itself.

So as we age, crises will come. Our identities will reform. We will engage with transformations in various aspects of our lives. But in all, to survive and thrive as older women we must reconstruct new meanings for ourselves and repurpose our lives. This we can do via the choices we make (what, when, where, and how we choose). Remember that we have that power of choice as we age and that our choice is the key that can open up reserves of dignity and well-being for us.

As women, our familiar roles can help us to bring some stability to our lives. As we age, we still stabilize our homes. We still do chores at home. We still take care of our loved ones (where we are able to). We still watch our favorites TV shows. We still love and laugh. We still gossip. We still clip coupons. All these familiar routines ultimately help us to hold our lives in place as we travel down the road of time.

Yet, if we must thrive as we age, we must learn new skills and acquire new habits. In old age our bodies and relationships would have gone through immense change. What worked in times past, what we used to do easily in the days of yore may no longer be easily possible or possible at all. Thus we need new understandings, new frameworks, new and better navigational know-hows and capabilities to be able to survive and thrive in this stage.

Most of us remember our younger versions. We remember our youth, our vitality, our beauty, our sexiness, our sexuality. We remember our oomph! And all of that (to different degrees) had been an integral part of our identity for decades. So how do you feel now as you watch all of this slowly but steadily fade? Disoriented? So how have you reacted? Have you taken it all in stride and pushed forward or have you developed a new relationship with a certain fellow named Denial?

What we must do is to develop a new perspective and attitude towards life. We must begin to see all of our experiences, all of our pains, joys and challenges at this stage as beautiful gifts (what life is made up of), each presenting us with an opportunity to learn and grow. In this guise we must welcome every experience (negative of positive). We must understand and welcome our fading or faded beauty, our physically weakened and restricted bodies, and our loss of social position, power and control. And basically we must construct these new experiences as valuable crucibles of knowledge from which we can learn new skills and capabilities.

We also need to be resilient to survive and thrive at this stage. And resilience is not fixed. You can pick it up. You can learn it just as you can learn to cook a Chinese dish or learn a new board game. We also need to keep growing in order to survive and thrive at this stage. But growth is evitable. Growth comes from a choice you make. And that choice is to choose to grow and to invest the necessary effort required to do so. It is either that, or you remain as small, as isolated and as introverted as you can be, fossilized in familiar but antiquated ideas. That is also a choice, your choice. In any event, we can still make the better choice of the two at any time. It is simply never too late to choose to grow.

We older women no longer enjoy the security and protection that youth and youthful healthiness had provided to us. In addition, we must now deal with a new set of cultural stereotypes and societal expectations. We, therefore, must craft for ourselves a space and place in this society with our own new goals and responsibilities. For one thing, we can each learn to be arbiters of our society's moral imagination. We can learn to be exemplary survivors amidst the roughest of currents. We can learn to be paragons of courage.

Old age comes with its joys and sufferings. All life stages do. But attitude and intentionality are the lords of this stage. With the right attitude, aging can be redemptive, but we must see and exploit the opportunities for growth that old age's peculiar challenges present to us. It is important that at all

31

times (in this life stage), that we remain focused about what kind of women we would like to become at this stage. So we must embrace both the suffering and the joys that come with this life stage, so that we can grow from them.

You cannot stop aging or old age, as you cannot stop the march of time. But even as old folks we can put ourselves in a desirable place via the power in our choices, our intentionality, our resilience, our attitude and plain old gratitude. These can enable us to navigate and adapt to the inevitable challenges and changes in this life stage.

We must not fear loss or suffering. There is, after all, recovery after loss. Most women who lose their life partners still recover and push ahead. Besides, suffering can also be advantageous because personal insufferability grows in the absence of suffering. Suffering also provides us with depth, with a certain emotional depth. It also increases our tolerance for pain, and it prepares and sharpens our resilience. Suffering also forces a new perspective on us that makes us to realize that a good day, a good hour, or even a good minute is a divine gift to be appreciated and savored. Without suffering we may fall into the mistake of taking many free and simple things for granted. With this understanding, you can see that almost everything can be and should be enjoyed!

Furthermore, suffering grants us the capacity to understand and feel compassion and gratitude. And suffering provides us with the necessary environment and impetus for growth. Growth requires, first, a brokenness, such that can come from suffering. So, yes, loss and suffering come with this life stage but so also do compassion, empathy, gratitude, understanding, wisdom and joy. And we can endeavor to become women who embody these traits and ideals.

Well-being may well reside on the obverse of catastrophe. That is the duality in our condition (actually it is the duality in the human condition). That is how life is. And we must meet this understanding with the contentment and wisdom that come with this life stage. Thus we can joyfully and successfully navigate, negotiate, survive and thrive as we journey down the path of time.

It can be fun.

It must be fun.

We shall make it fun!

CHAPTER 2: THE LAY OF THE LAND

KEY TAKEAWAYS

- Aging and old age is an inevitable fate waiting to befall everyone. The elderly among us should serve as constant reminders of this life stage that awaits all of us.

- Ageism is a social disease that most old American women suffer from. The suffering from this disease is worse than the suffering that comes from aging itself.

- Physical attractiveness is overvalued in terms of its use as a defining feature for women in America. Old women find it difficult to maintain the generally accepted young-looking and slender bodies socially expected of women.

- The overall pressure from society on older women to look young and to fit a certain ideal image in order to keep their jobs, makes older women to opt for cosmetic surgery (some of which can be invasive and dangerous). It also forces old women to dye their hair.

- Where the behaviors and misbehaviors of younger people may be excused lightly, those of older people are often attributed to old age, senility and often draw derision.

- Several role reversals come to play as aging sets in. Our children move into power and refuse to take our advice while our doctors and supervisors become younger than us. This can be disconcerting and disorienting for older folks.

- There are several things we can do to remove the stereotype attached to older women in our society. Some of those things include (i) educating the public about the negative effects of the stereotype on the lives of older people; (ii) reminding the younger ones that everyone will eventually grow old one day; (iii) resolving not to be involved in self criticism and criticism of others; (iv) and refraining from making negative comments concerning old appearances.

- According to Margaret Mead, an ideal society is one that has a place for all categories of human gift. But does our society have any place for the gifts of aging women?

SUMMARY

A young girl walked up to me one afternoon while I was sitting in the park, bird watching. She asked to look at the pictures in the bird guide I had with me. I obliged her. After looking at the various pictures in my book, she took a good look at me and then asked me with all sincerity: *"where do old ladies come from?"* To her young mind, old people were a different species of humans. But we, most certainly, are not! We are still humans like everyone else! Old age is a life stage that we will all reach if we remain alive. It is inevitable. The sight of all the old people around us should serve as a constant reminder of the unavoidability of old age.

There is an emotional/ cultural distancing from old people in our society. While this affects both genders, women are more vulnerable and more negatively affected. Most old American women suffer from ageism, a social disease, worse than aging itself. The society mocks our sexuality, derides our skin and silences our voices. We feel so useless in this society that places more value on the young and the beautiful, and barely has any time for the old.

Because of the negative construction that the society and our culture have assigned to old women, a lot of women refuse to admit the fact that they are old. By doing so they are merely refusing to identify with those negative constructions which society has heaped on old age. The glitterati (including the movie, fashion, television, style, advertising industries, etc.) have abandoned old women. A recent study revealed that old female characters have been missing in family films. As a result of the premium placed on attractiveness in America, women are expected to have young looks and slender bodies, a defining feature that is largely absent in old women.

Nevertheless, older people have certain distinguishing features, although they have unfortunately gone unnoticed. For example older people often have the ability to connect. They are largely peace lovers and peace makers. They are custodians, caretakers and emotional processors. But unfortunately old folks (particularly old women) are often pressurized to look young and they end up doing things that are not naturally convenient for them. For instance, in order to keep their jobs and partners, older women often opt to undergo cosmetic surgery or to dye their hair.

Older women are often considered to have lost competence even regarding the most basic functions and roles. And as a result people tend to inflict unsolicited help and advice on us, even when we are still quite capable and doing just fine. In addition, the use of the words "we" or "our" or "us" on older women is disrespectful, discounting and demoralizing. This often happens when people think they are being kind to us and they say things like: *"Hello Mrs. Smith, how are we today?"* or *"Did we take all our medications today?"* or *"Oh, that's a little too heavy for us, perhaps we could manage something lighter?"* and so on. These are all painful words and expressions that infantilize us!

Aging to women is also a disempowering experience. We experience role reversals that are both confusing and painful. Younger people gradually assume all the positions of power and enjoy all the prominence, societal acceptance and prestige, while we are basically kicked to the curb, left out, stunned by it all and wondering what happened. Even our lawyers, doctors, and supervisors who used to be much older than us, are now much younger than us, perhaps, decades younger than us. And our children who used to depend on us for most things, would have now matured into their own independence and power. Mostly and very painfully they wouldn't even want our assistance or advice anymore.

There is a danger for old women. If we begin to internalize the negative, anti-age comments and constructions heaped upon us by society, we may unconsciously begin to act and become what they call us; relegating our values.

Industrialization has a way of negatively affecting the relationship between older people, parents and their wards all over the world. One way to re-conceptualize the lost relationship between the young and the old is to begin to see ourselves as interdependent beings and not as the young wanting to be independent while the old fear being dependent. We need to understand each other. We need each other.

Good interaction between generations/ age groups leads to a flourishing culture. Also via the interaction, different age groups can inspire and energize one another. When we allow an unnecessary gap to exist between the age groups, misunderstandings amass and great potentials are lost.

Some young people are caring and each time I experience this, I'm almost moved to tears. In the face of this, there are old women who go unnoticed and uncared for by younger people and this comes with some negative impact. This can lead to older people becoming apathetic and detached, behaving anyhow they want since no one cares, anyway. They may deteriorate to becoming mere silent observers of society, no longer caring about their appearances, skipping events they are not interested in, and feeling as if they have the freedom to do as they want. This is not good especially if it comes from a feeling of being uninvited, unaccepted, discounted and irrelevant.

I interviewed Suzanna, an old woman in my community and her perspective on ageism is the same thing. She hid her age from others at the place of work because disclosing it won't compromise her relationships and prospects at work. She felt less confident when giving presentations in recent times because of her age. She was afraid of dying. She was also afraid of leaving her job because it was the only thing that gave her voice and recognition, as most other retired people were no longer being heard from.

It is possible to secure respect for older women and claim back our power. (i) First we must create the awareness and educate people about the negative effects of their stereotypes on us. (ii) We must also create the awareness and educate them about the universality and inevitability of old age, as we all will become old someday. (iii) We can also decide to accept ourselves as we are and stop criticizing others and ourselves. (iv) We can also dismantle ageism through posters, letters, protests and so on. There are several things we can do to push down all the negative policies and practices against old people and reunite ourselves with our society.

If a society prefers the young because of their present beauty and youthful looks, that society must remember that every one of its members will eventually get old (as long as they remain alive). So everyone is bound to taste the same bitter pill of constructed irrelevance that we face today.

But, it doesn't have to be that way. It is still very possible for us to discover new ways to adapt to age changes in order to continue to remain empowered and engaged in society. It is our duty to teach our society to care for our aging bodies and about us.

CHAPTER 3: THE WORN BODY

KEY TAKEAWAYS

- Ageing comes with various challenges and changes in health and lifestyle. We experience changes in all our different body parts including changes in our sex lives.

- No matter how agile you may have been in your younger days, your body will eventually give you the signal that it can no longer do those things that it used to be able to do. Even where there is a will, the body will say, there is no way.

- Aging affects the mind. Some of the symptoms include loss of memory. But while older people may forget details here and there, they still excel at retrieving memorable stories and events from the past.

- Older people have a more pronounced ability at connecting and being distinctive.

- Aging mellows us and induces us to show kindness to older people as we appreciate our parents and what they had gone through.

- Irrespective of the burden being carried by older folks, besides learning to cope with aging, we can also make light of old he and aging, have our fun with it and laugh at its expense.

- Creating a healing package for ourselves is the way to find our happiness. We can develop our prescription for good health by paying attention to our relationships, hobbies, nutrition, exercise and even gratitude.

- Instead of complaining and seeing ourselves as being unfortunate because of our challenges, pains and travails with aging and old age, we can learn to habitually relapse into gratitude for everything.

- My grandmother used to say that she had no choice about her leukemia sickness but that it was up to her to control how she dealt with it. You must not always dwell on the condition of your health. It is possible to wave aside your health concerns at times and think of something more interesting and fun to occupy your mind.

- In spite of our aging pains and worn out bodies, we can find a way to appreciate other things around us. We can still discover and experience beauty, joy, peace, etc.

SUMMARY

Pia, a friend, always likes to take visitors to her study to show them old pictures of her as proof that she had once been young and vibrant too like other young people.

As we grow older, we experience a lot of different physical changes in our body. We experience changes in our teeth, bones, skin, vision, body shape, taste and smell. We can no longer bear cold as much because of our thinning skin. Our thinning skin also causes us to bruise easily. We fight to gain coordination and balance when we walk or stand. And everything just sags and droops (neck, cheeks, arms, eyes, etc,)

Aging affects different people differently. For instance, some people may become more sexually active while others may distance themselves from that idea at this point of life. Other factors such as loneliness, isolation or illness also affect our sexuality as we age.

Sylvia and Lewis are old couples living in Texas. They are in charge of their two grandchildren; their only daughter's kids. Lenore, is their only daughter who they tried raising well but who later fell into drug use and other social vices. Though alive, they are not aware of Lenore's whereabouts. This causes pain in both old couples who spend their nights in tears as a consequence. The couple has been living together without sex for years and Sylvia's health is not helping matters.

Sometimes, the desire to be agile and to do things the way you used to in your younger days will surface, but the body will tell you that such is no longer possible. Aging makes people give up on certain physical pleasures and fun (e.g. playing tennis or other similar physical games).

Aging also affects the mind. If you were able to combine several things in the past, you may find that you can no longer do so any more. Also, aging brings about the tendency of experiencing memory loss and the inability of learning new things, unlike during our younger days.

As we age, we tend to appreciate older people and show kindness to them. While I couldn't stand the talk about health and lack of sleep when I was younger, I now understand the challenges older people face as they advance in age. I didn't take health insurance while growing up despite my poor health and eating habits. I never knew that I'll also have to do cataract surgery and have other health challenges like the older people around me when I was much younger. I have a total different view about health now.

The situation of older folks is not as bad as it may seem. Apart from learning to cope with aging, we can also make light of it, have our fun and laugh at its expense.

Kestrel is an aging woman who grew up in the rural Washington. Her father was an alcoholic and also abusive. She grew up to become hard and defensive.

She grew up to hate relationships and maintain just few, trusting no one. Unfortunately, she inherited the drinking trait from her father. On one visit to her doctor, she was advised to drop drinking alcohol and to instead drink milk. She managed to stop drinking alcohol but it was difficult. Because of her health, she had no other choice than to quit. She eventually found solace in tonic water combined with lime

When my doctor told me about the state of my hand that I shouldn't write or carry any heavy thing, I was a bit devastated. I started looking at people when they use their hands and appreciate how healthy they were. I later discovered there were other things I could do like swimming, reading, talking and so on.

On one occasion during the period my doctor asked me to give my hands rest, I went to a dinner with some friends and complained to them about my hands. One of them pointedly told me to appreciate my hands for serving me thus far and the fact that I could still talk with them.

CHAPTER 4: INTENSITY AND POIGNANCY

KEY TAKEAWAYS

- People in their sixties often think the way they did in their forties. However their sixty-year-old bodies can no longer act the way it did when they were in their forties.

- Each time I think of time, what I see is a picture of an old movie and a page in a calendar with dates that are easily blown off by the wind.

- I love poems because I have discovered that poems are the only thing or language that can effectively express the depth and complex nature of my feelings.

- The knowledge of the finiteness of the time we have left affects our decisions and perspectives.

- The knowledge of the finiteness of the time we have left induces us to become more focused on joy, and on taking our pleasures now.

- As we age, we have less experience of anxiety and anger.

- The blessing of knowing that our final journey on earth is closer, is gratitude. We become grateful for the gift of life. We enjoy every moment because there is nothing like small pleasures. There is nothing like those little magical moments (M&Ms) that life routinely and constantly throws to us. Yes, they are there! They are always there! Train yourself to recognize these M&Ms and enjoy and savor every last one of them. They are the "unpains", the "unsufferings", the antitheses to the tribulations and pains of aging, old age, Being and the human condition itself. So pet a cat should you run into one in the street. What! You exclaim! Well, for more explanation you might want to also read Rule 12 in Jordan Peterson's book, *"12 Rules for life: An Antidote to Chaos"*.

SUMMARY

Emma is a sixty eight years old woman who has been married to Chris for over forty years. They have three children who have been married but divorced though two of them have remarried. One day, Emma invited her grand kids; four of them, to her house during the holidays. She took them out and had a great time with them. But, she couldn't believe how fast time had flown. She couldn't imagine that her grandchildren who were babies just like yesterday had grown so big! And then she also realized that her own children were now in their thirties and forties. She also marveled at how quickly she had grown so old considering that she was just a kid only a few years ago. She also pondered, albeit ruefully, that even her grandchildren would soon become old women too.

Each time I think of time, I imagine an old movie with a calendar in the background, and the wind blowing the calendar pages away, slowly, one after another.

In our sixties, we have this feeling of doing certain things for the last time. Such thoughts make us view those last moments as being poignant. At this stage of life, we resort to the use of single words in describing our complex feelings, which are often intertwined with emotions such as fear, sadness, sorrow, bitterness and similar mixed feelings.

Frank and Frances have been family friends for several years and they often come visiting. But, the last visit, (which we probably knew was going to be the last, although we couldn't utter it) was memorable. Unlike previous visits, we couldn't do much outdoor activities because of the stroke Frank was suffering from. When it was time for him to depart, we hugged him goodbye, knowing that it might really be the last goodbye, considering his age.

There is always change in our decisions and perspectives as we reflect and perceive the shortness of how much time we have left due to age. As we grow older, we have fewer feelings of anxiety and anger. Not because we have less tragedies but because of the coping skills we have developed.

Immediately after birth, we begin to sense that death is inevitable but as we approach it through aging, we go to it with a deeper emotional experience, a fearless resignation.

CHAPTER 5: CAREGIVING

- Old women take up care-giving tasks for their friends or loved ones. While it can bring fulfillment, it's also fraught with stress at this stage of life.

- Care-giving entails putting aside your personal needs and sacrificing your time for the welfare of others.

- Forty to seventy percent of caregivers experience depression while forty percent find the task of aregiving to be stressful.

- We experience happiness in various ways. But when we have contentment, it is also happiness.

- If the definition of work is the creation of good things on earth, then care-giving is the best job ever.

- While it is good to take care of others, we must balance it up by taking care of ourselves too.

SUMMARY

Joel and Crystal were husband and wife who managed an ice cream parlor together. Jim and I used to do many community projects and other things together with Joel and Crystal. One day, I saw Crystal pushing Joel in a wheelchair. Joel had had a stroke and could no longer take care of himself completely. Crystal was obviously taking care of Joel. When we sat down, Crystal narrated her experience to me, and it was not pleasant at all. She told me that she had discovered that there was a great difference between when they were much younger and now that they had become old. She had to be her husband's caregiver after his stroke that affected many areas of his life. Crystal started doing alone what she and Joel used to do together.

Crystal had become a caregiver to her husband, a demanding task. While care-giving can give us a sense of fulfillment, enabling us to be useful to the people close to us, it can also be demanding on our health. It's like the women of our generation were raised to be self sacrificing. Many of them are currently engaged in this selfless task.

Such is the nature of care-giving. Care-giving is one of the tasks that give us purpose and meaning in life, but, unfortunately, caregivers are not well paid. And there are other caregivers who are neither paid at all, nor even acknowledged for their efforts.

Ardith works as a graphic artist and also cares for her mother who has refused to go to a care facility. As a consequence, Ardith sacrifices most of the time she is supposed to spend with her husband, caring for her mother instead.

There is the need for self protection, self care plans and setting healthy limits when taking care of people, as care-giving can encroach and sometimes take over our private lives for a long time. We can also involve other friends to give helping hands as we give care. Encouraging visits and welcoming visitors to the place of care-giving can also be helpful.

Willow and Saul had all things going well until her husband was diagnosed with Parkinson's. She was unprepared to be a caregiver and consequently she resorted to complaining. Though it wasn't easy at first, but she gradually accepted her fate and grew into her new role.

CHAPTER 6: SWEPT AWAY

KEY TAKEAWAYS

- To properly help someone to face death, ensure that their wishes around dying and death are clear. This is because if they lose capacity and are no longer able to decide for themselves, and if you must decide for them, you will need adequate information about their wishes in order to make good decisions for them.

- Thus it would be necessary to procure the relevant powers of attorney, a will, directives concerning major issues in the person's life, and instructions concerning funeral choices, etc.

- But most importantly a general family understanding of the requirements for the final care for the person in question needs to have been established. This would require that a series of conversations must have been had over time between the persons in question and members of her family.

- The fear that most people have about death is not of physical pain. It is rather fear of the emotional pain and an aftermath that is shrouded in mystery.

- Hospices can be very helpful in the process. Generally, hospice workers can nurse the emotional, physical and spiritual pain that comes dying. Hospices encourage patients to accept death and to meet it with resoluteness, fearlessness, a sense of fulfillment and dignity.

- Hospices counsel that there are five basic conversations that most dying prsons want to have with their loved ones. They are: (i) asking for forgiveness (ii) granting and communicating forgiveness (iii) expressions of love for and from, (iv) expressions of gratitude and thankfulness to and from, and (v) saying goodbye. Hospices encourage and facilitate the holding of these conversations.

- Although we are encouraged to stay around our loved ones when they are dying, most people, nevertheless, prefer to die when they are alone (in the absence of their family members). They feel it is best to avoid the emotional pains of their family members being present, preferring instead to silently drift away into death when no one is there.

- True grief hardly goes away. It's not easy to forget. But we learn to live with and manage it.

- Grief is both complex and long. Although it never ends, it can be ameliorated.

SUMMARY

Jenny had a good time caring for her parents before they died. She called, Skyped and texted them regularly. When her mother said she was ready to leave this world because of her unbearable pains, Jenny organized a special weekend for her mother to be with her children and grandchildren. Her mother was happy and relaxed. The following Tuesday, she died. Jenny then took her father to live with her family and took very good care of him. But he too died after one month.

Our society does not encourage discussions about death. If one dares discuss it, one is usually accused of being morbid. Because of this, we miss sharing a lot of things, a lot of information with our dying loved ones. But we can help others to face death gracefully. In that case, we need to be clear about their specific desires and wishes. We should encourage those who are alert to make their own decisions. But where we are to take up the decision-making for them, we ought to have adequate information about their wishes in order to make proper decisions for them.

Women who choose to move to hospices end up living longer than their male counterparts. This is because women embrace more of the emotional discussions and they are more open to alternative treatment methods.

Mavis did everything to make the last days of Rick, her husband, worthwhile (after he was diagnosed of a deadly disease). She cared so much for him and after

55

he died she was shrouded in deep sadness and loneliness. But she learnt several lessons from the experience. For one she realized that when it mattered, it turned out that she was competent and patient enough to take care of a dying loved one and make them comfortable. She also learned that sometimes it is best to forgo the long term and to just take things one day at a time.

People adopt different rituals to help themselves heal after losing a loved one. For me, I write eulogies about the person and I try to remember the great moments we shared together.

CHAPTER 7: LONELINESS AND SOLITUDE

KEY TAKEAWAYS

- Irrespective of the way our lives are structured, we are destined to live alone as we age.

- Loneliness is synonymous with life. Right from childhood to adulthood, we experience loneliness.

- A lot of people's lifestyles have been affected one way or the other by the decisions of friends or people close to them when they move to distant locations. They feel so alone and unable to cope with life again.

- The reason why some old women feel lonely at their final stage is that they had placed a poor value on cultivating relationships in their younger days and so never cultivated any. Instead of cultivating relationships, some of these women occupied their time with travelling, career, business, etc.

- Friendship (especially with neighbors) contributes to our happiness.

- Since loneliness is inevitable at old age, we can leverage on it to take care of ourselves and also reach out to people around us.

- There are several ways we can cope with loneliness. One outstanding secret of happiness is discovering an activity we enjoy doing while alone.

- We can transform our loneliness to solitude by using our skills to nourish ourselves and foster strong connections with those surrounding us.

SUMMARY

Carla, one of my friends, looked back and wished the days she spent with her children could come back because she felt alone. As we grow older (especially women) we have a mix of solitary and lonely experiences.

Holly didn't lose any family member to death, but the only family she had (her daughter, her son-in-law, and her grand children) were moving to another location 1000 miles away (a job transfer). It was unbearable. There would be loneliness and solitude. The separation left a lasting grief in Holly.

Mona is a work-from-home mom whose social circle is limited to social media and her work clients. She lacks relationships with any local friends. She is lonely. Even though she had online relationships, she realized that it is important to have physical friendships, as friendships contribute to happiness.

As we age loneliness becomes inevitable but we can find a way of connecting with people in our community by joining various groups. We can take advantage of our loneliness to nurture ourselves and to extend friendship to others.

We can develop several activities to help us cope with loneliness, such as listening to music, rendering help or visiting others.

CHAPTER 8:
UNDERSTANDING OURSELVES

KEY TAKEAWAYS

- To know yourself while you are aging implies knowing your personal needs and having a strong sense of who you are in changing situations.

- Understanding ourselves makes us skillful at distinguishing between acting on impulse, and acting according to our real self.

- Before jumping at the opportunity of accepting anyone who needs our services, we ought to allow ourselves the choice and opportunity to think and decide for ourselves whether to accept the opportunity or not.

- We must know how to protect both our space and our time. Time management isn't for the faint heart.

- We must know our personal needs and be assertive enough to demand them even if they would make others uncomfortable.

- Since I discovered the power of simply saying "no", I have refused to accept any unpleasant situation where I feel cheated, neglected, disrespected or abused. I simply say "no" and walk away.

- As we age, we need the special skills of self protection and self knowledge to prevent constant denial.

SUMMARY

Life is constantly changing for everyone so getting to know ourselves can be somehow complicated. As humans, we have a limited level of knowledge. That is why we can't understand ourselves fully. We can engage in several things like discussing our concerns with therapists or friends, walking, reading, meditating in order to explore ourselves and discover who we are.

Contrary to what our culture teaches us, we must identify what we desire and go all out for it. Women usually find it difficult to say "no". Instead they use phrases like "maybe", "later", "that's okay", "I'll think about it", and so on. Women are not trained to literally say "no". We must therefore be able to summon up the courage to walk away from any space/situation that we don't want to be in.

CHAPTER 9: MAKING INTENTIONAL CHOICES

KEY TAKEAWAYS

- We have the freedom to intentionally choose our response to the situations around us. We have that power of choice. And remember that our attitudes trump our circumstances.

- Happiness is not only a choice it is also a set of skills. If we decide to be happy at all times, then we must develop the different types of skills that are necessary to achieve such a goal.

- We should devise several strategies for calming ourselves. One way is to take charge of our internal dialogue. We could say to ourselves: "it's not time to worry yet", "tomorrow is another day", "it could be worse", "everyone makes mistakes", "it's not the end of the world" etc. Internalizing these types of dialogue can help us to keep things in perspective.

- The tragedies that we experience are good teachers and connectors for us. They compel us to learn, to trust and to connect with others.

- We need to be intentional about how we spend our time and money. We have that power of choice. That choice is up to us.

- There is wisdom in choosing to live a life that allows us to grow, flourish and love.

SUMMARY

Marlene grew up in a poor family with an alcoholic father. Apart from being poor, she is also epileptic. She had two children. She also divorced her husband and became a single mom, shutting her heart against men until she met her current boyfriend.

She had known that things would be pretty tough from the beginning and she had braced herself to face them. She had also resolved to enjoy her life. Instead of allowing her epileptic situation and poverty to shape her life, she decided to choose joy and love intentionally.

We can choose to be happy or hopeless. Both are self fulfilling prophecies. The difference between the way "A" reacts to an unpleasant situation and the way "B" reacts depends on their attitudes as well as the coping capacities that they may or may not have developed.

Freedom is the opposite of reactivity (acting on every emotion or impulse that comes on our way). Making conscious choices according to our deepest values gives us freedom.

When Kestrel's mother, Evelyn, was diagnosed with stage III cancer, Kestrel left everything to be with her mother during and after the surgery and chemotherapy. Kestrel's mother loved the time her daughter stayed with her.

Note that how we spend our time matters a lot. Consider spending your time taking care of relationships or volunteering for a project.

From our twenties to forties, our schedules revolve around work, children and other personal matters. Time does not only spend us, it leaves us spent. But as we age, we should begin to take better decisions about how we spend our time. It is preferable to spend our time pursuing our inherent gifts, than to just watch television all day.

We should be able to distinguish between what we want and what we need. We often have enough when our needs are met. Thus the secret of feeling wealthy is the ability to enjoy what you have plus the ability to welcome the contentment that follows.

We should consciously choose to spend our time on things that will make us love, flourish and grow. There are certain choices that we can make now that will eventually give us a sense of fulfillment, happiness and pride on our deathbeds.

CHAPTER 10: BUILDING A GOOD DAY

KEY TAKEAWAYS

- For you to be happy, you need to learn ways of structuring each day to be meaningful, productive and rich in memorable events.

- We can get the needed courage to face each new day if we create and schedule events ahead, for each new day, that is, events and activities we can look forward to. It is those planned activities that will give the new day that desired sense of purpose. Planning ahead and envisioning a new day speckled with the new day's events will give us the energy with which to face each day and its challenges.

- Note that we can and should have periodic appointment-free days. We can also dedicate days in which we will make do without cell phones, social media or internet surfing.

- Instead of always thinking long term, sometimes, when the times are tough, think short term. Take it one day at a time.

- We need self monitoring to avoid too much hunger, anger, loneliness and tiredness. Breathing slowly but deeply helps control our degree of reactivity. There is also a place for mini vacations in our lives. It helps us to relieve stress.

- We need to develop many good habits that will help us to cope with stress. If we do not intentionally choose to do this, we will, in the alternative, develop bad and self destructive habits (such as smoking, over eating, drinking, watching too much television and so on) just so we can cope with stress.

SUMMARY

Building a good day starts with our decision to make good choices covering our behavior, emotion and thought. Our days can be specially crafted with provisions made for memorable and healthy activities; coping techniques against stress; and spending time with friends, family members and other loved ones. We ought to cultivate a lifestyle of humor and a "Teflon" attitude for each day, irrespective of what the day brings.

There is nothing like magical future. The way we spend our time defines us. And the future is actually determined today, just as today is the anticipated future of yesterday and past years.

It's a bit like writing. Just as you can delete or add words, sentences, paragraphs and even whole chapters, you can equally delete or add certain chores or activities from or to your daily schedule.

We can and should give ourselves treats and take a break often (even if it is mini breaks). This means we should not overcrowd our day with appointments. Space must always be reserved for relaxation.

Sylvia accepted her doctor's advice to visit the pain clinic. Megan, her therapist, gave Sylvia several tips to which she adhered and her life improved. Her happiness also extended to her husband. She planned her schedules for each day such as time for back exercises, swimming, meeting with other women in the church, journaling etc. She also took time to rate her pains. This helped her a great deal.

We can take a cue from Sylvia. We should also rate our own stress. Give your stress points on a scale of 0 – 10. Obviously you would begin to address them from the 10s all the way down to 1.

We should also learn to manage our daily expectations. If we make our expectations too high about anything or if we over-expect our day to be free of problems, our disappointment (and the resulting stress) will be higher if the reverse is what we eventually experience on the day in question.

We should generally operate from a default mindset of not expecting too much from people and life. This is because everything about life tends to gravitate towards problem solving.

While the beginning of a day matters, the way we end our day is also a vital part of how we spent that day. As we await sleep, we can reflect on the happenings of the day, places visited, things learned and other happy, memorable moments.

.

CHAPTER 11: CREATING COMMUNITY

KEY TAKEAWAYS

- Old age is the best time to create something in our community. It is also an appropriate stage during which we should offer our accumulated wealth of experience to our generation before we depart.

- But as we render service to people around us, there is the need for caution. We must accept only those duties that allow us adequate time to reconstitute and rest. The work we choose to do should not disrupt us from still engaging in those things that we love to do. Whatever we volunteer for must give us room to continue doing what we love doing.

- Instead of wallowing in the feeling of hopelessness concerning the challenges confronting your community, you can instead take a proactive step and organize a group that can advocate the way forward.

- The most essential thing is that we should be able to identify our talents and strengths and determine how best they can be harnessed to serve our community.

- Here's an open secret. Old women working together towards a goal or project in their community have often discovered such an engagement to be a surprise antidote to their despair. Involving oneself in community projects is a self confidence and self esteem booster, a pathway to feeling good about oneself.

SUMMARY

Several people have found that their old age is a special time for them to bequeath to the world all that they have learned from it. The period of old age is a time to give our talents and share our knowledge and skills with others. We all have something we can offer. It could be time. We could offer our time by visiting a lonely neighbor or we could render one service or the other to or community and to mankind.

Nora and Roger created a community park for their community before they died. After creating the park (and while they were still alive) they found fulfillment when they saw people visiting and having a nice time in the park that they had created. And even long after they had died and disappeared from the community, the park is still there and it is still relevant and still of great use to the community. The idea of building a community park came to Nora and Roger when they discovered that there was no park in their community. And so they decided to build one. You can do something similar. You can bequeath something of value to your community that could still be relevant and useful to the community even long after you've passed on.

There is always something we can offer to the people around us and to the community at large. Working on a project in groups is better than working on a project singlehandedly. But when we decide to work as a group, we should seek out people who we can work with, including those that we like and those who are likely to cooperate with us.

Forming a group is easy. You can send for friends who share your ideas or who are experts to join the group. Another thing is that while it is good to form a new group, we must also know that joining an existing group can be an easier way for us to contribute to our community.

CHAPTER 12: CRAFTING RESPLENDENT NARRATIVES

KEY TAKEAWAYS

- Hear this and do not forget it. No matter what the past has been we may not be able to change it. But we may still be able to change our stories because it is not the histories of our lives that influence us, rather it is the narratives that we keep repeating to ourselves concerning that history.

- It may take time but we can painstakingly train ourselves to reason and think of stories that give us room to flourish. These are stories of courage, past achievements, celebration, kindness and so on. These types of stories have ways of giving us courage.

- No matter the pressing situation; no matter how dire the circumstances, we all still have good stories that we can uncover.

- For example, we can craft positive stories from the past such as the songs we sang when we were young, places we visited, memorable and pleasurable experiences we had and so on. No matter how bad one's life has been, remembering the music and sounds of your past can have a tremendous healing effect on you, flooding your soul with joy.

- My most unique story is how to help people. It has helped me to offer assistance to others at various times.

- It is easier to turn our tragedies to comedies when we laugh at our past failures and mistakes.

SUMMARY

It is not always easy to change our past but we have the power to change our stories. It is not the past or the history associated with it that influences us, rather it is the perspectives and narratives that we keep repeating about that past that influences us. There are many different positive ways in which we can think about ourselves and others. We can reconstruct, revisit and recompose our most painful and unpleasant experiences, turning them into positive narratives for our internal dialogue.

Sometimes, it might be difficult to craft good stories but the people around us such as our spouses and friends can help remind us of past positive events. As we age, we tend to have a better understanding of situations and better ways of interpreting people's actions from a more mature point of view. We tend to take things a little less personal.

I have been to several places that have given me a lot of pleasant memories. Good stories often build good lives so we need to reexamine our stories with the aim of focusing on acceptance, resilience and clarity. This focus will help us grow in joy and confidence.

CHAPTER 13: ANCHORING IN GRATITUDE

KEY TAKEAWAYS

- Gratitude is a skill of life which can be improved through practice. We can make it a healthy habit through which we can learn to find things to love, appreciate and enjoy in spite of the tough circumstances around us.

- We are wise when we can recollect and appreciate small gifts, events and things.

- The most cheerful people I have noticed in life are those with histories of serious hardship.

SUMMARY

Dr. Zhivago is one of the characters I read about in Pasternak's book. He focuses on the beautiful aspect of life irrespective of the unpleasant situation facing him. I have personally adopted his style as one of my stress coping skills.

Oftentimes, it is the less privileged that show gratitude more than those who have the better things of life. Contentment is one great thing that leads to a happy life. We can savor life and have great joy out of life if we can wake up from our airplane mode of being inattentive to becoming attentive to the things happening around us.

I interviewed Sally and her perspective to life challenged me. I learned to put my problems in perspective after interacting with her. Despite the burden she was bearing, she was still cheerful and grateful.

CHAPTER 14: TRAVEL COMPANIONS

KEY TAKEAWAYS

- Friendships hold our lives in place as we age. In fact, it is of topmost priority but our culture will not teach us this.

- For friends, we can choose women who will give us room to grow; women who we feel comfortable in their presence. We should make friends with women with whom we share same values.

SUMMARY

Women are known to have always worked together (from raising children to searching for food and other forms of doing things together). Though this lifestyle still holds, in this century, it requires commitment and planning. We tend to be distant from each other and also find it difficult to stay connected.

There are several benefits attached to friendships. Friends can encourage us, make us relax, and lend us a shoulder upon which we can cry. Friends can comfort us and help us pull through various unpleasant experiences.

Carrie's husband left her at over sixty years of age for a student of his. She felt so bad she decided that she was going to be sad and lonely for six months before she would start a new phase of life. She had some old friends who were always there for her to encourage her and cheer her up. That is the power of friendship.

Some of our women groups were formed when we were strong and energetic at age thirties and forties. We still meet till date to share past memories but our talks are limited to "organ recitals" (issues concerning our health), retirement and other similar aging discussions. Nevertheless, I always feel better when we meet.

CHAPTER 15: CO-CAPTAINS

KEY TAKEAWAYS

- It is not those with perfect relationships that stay married, rather it is those who decided to commit and stick to it no matter the circumstances.

- Couples who thrive in their marriages are those that give their partner both the social and emotional space to grow.

- Another trick for a happy marriage is to hold your tongue. Do not say everything just exactly as you have them in your thoughts. Before you rattle off, pause and take a couple of deep breaths. You may eventually realize that you needn't say whatever it was that you wanted to say, after all.

- There is nothing nearly as exquisite and special like getting married and staying together till old age. Such is a gift of security. It is just wonderful and invaluable to have a reliable and loving spouse you can lean on all through your life.

SUMMARY

Emma met her husband, Chris, when she was nineteen. He was in college at the time and had hopes of becoming an engineer. But he later dropped out of school to take care of Emma when she became pregnant. They have had their ups and downs. He is now an old man. But she has a certain tenderness for him, and he for her. Theirs has been a long-term marriage which has survived based on experiences they learnt "on the job" and their commitment to stay married.

Commitment makes couples stay married and not because they have a perfect relationship. Marriages become successful when communication between couples is positive.

Because of the possibility of change as people grow, there is also the tendency for them to learn and develop entirely new interest from earlier ones.

The success of a marriage can be threatened when it is just one partner that is growing instead of the two growing together. Such couples would certainly grow apart instead of together. The ideal situation in marriages involves couples growing together and co-creating together.

Women are known to initiate most divorce cases. The most common complaint has always been that their spouse was controlling or that they do not receive enough attention/commitment from their spouse.

CHAPTER 16: THE LIFEBOAT OF FAMILY

KEY TAKEAWAYS

- As good as the family unit is to mankind, it can have both positive and negative effects on us. It can give the happiest moment and deepest pain.

- No matter how complex our family is and no matter how difficult to manage our family members are, we can always get one or two among them that we get along with and love.

- When we remember those who love us, we feel comfort and security. There is also the feeling of gratitude to those who have helped us.

- There are various things we can explore to connect us with our family history (e.g. family photo albums and visiting our ancestral homeland).

SUMMARY

Aging makes us curious about our family relationships and history. It is a stage during which we appreciate the family unit more. Families are important. It is our family that gives us that authentic basis of our identity, knowing that we belong to a group of people who also belong to us. A desirable family is one that is like a circle of trees, which protects us from both cold and wind.

It is not likely that we will get along with every member of our family but we can select and relate with a sibling or two who are dependable and who share the same values with us. And even if we don't have direct family members, we can adopt a family from among our friends and women groups.

By exploring your family photo album and visiting the place of your birth, you would be digging into your family history. This can imbue you with a sense of history and oneness with your ancestors who you would be joining some day.

CHAPTER 17:
GRANDCHILDREN

KEY TAKEAWAYS

- What I learned from my grandmother, I'm gradually imparting in my grandchildren.

- We can ponder what we want to teach our grandchildren; activities that will make them happy and other ways that we can help to prepare them to face the complications of this world.

- Our stories help our grandchildren develop perspective, point of view and identity, which will help them shape their understanding of experiences that they will face all through their lives.

- As our grandchildren grow up, we will need to make several adjustments. There are often role reversals. A time might come when we stay quieter and give less advice.

SUMMARY

Sylvia initially thought the presence of her grandchildren was burdensome but when she studied their uniqueness, she realized how lucky she was to have them. Not all grandmothers are this lucky. Apart from having badly behaved grandchildren, some experience distant relationship or estrangement from their own kids thus making their grandchildren unreachable to them.

Unlike when we tried shaping and forming our direct children to be like us, our grandchildren are accepted to be themselves. Children love doing tasks without being timed and interrupted. Schools and parents do not have such grace but as grandmothers, we can give our grandchildren the opportunity to be themselves.

I know my grandchildren's best food and I try to make it available for them. Children love stories and we can tell them different stories about their parents and other experiences we had when growing up.

Grandchildren that are between the ages of 3 and 10 can be fun to be with. Although the reality is that when our grandchildren become teenagers, their friends and other teenager activities can replace the love of grandmothers in their heart. This is because the role of grandmother is dynamic. As children cross from being kids to teenagers, their perspectives to life and love for things change too. Grandmothers, therefore, need to exercise caution and be ready to adjust to suit their grandchildren's changes.

CHAPTER 18: MOON RIVER: AUTHENTICITY AND SELF-ACCEPTANCE

KEY TAKEAWAYS

- By stopping to worry excessively about what others think of us, we are moving to discover our true selves.

- Authenticity means several things to several people. But, in all, it is the ability to accept and do what we are comfortable doing without being afraid of others or pleasing them.

- Self acceptance makes us less ambitious for prestige and recognition.

SUMMARY

As we grow older, we need to accept set boundaries and discover our true selves. There is nothing as powerful as discovering your true self. I stood in my way of being a better me when I had this constant quest to improve myself. When we learn to be good to that baby in us, we extend care and love to others.

CHAPTER 19: THE LONG VIEW

KEY TAKEAWAYS

- I have interacted with many people in this journey of life and they have helped shape my life.

- Besides outside influence, our immediate family has great influence on us. My maternal grandmother taught me to be selfless and think of others first but I've learned to think of myself more in the past decade.

SUMMARY

The best teacher of perspective is time, if we work at understanding our personal experiences. An examination of our life will often present both good and bad memories. In the midst of these differences, there are still things we loved doing when we were children that we still do now. This is called continuity. However, there are also things that you did when you were young that you probably can't bring yourself to doing again, because time has changed passed and changed many things.

In addition, even while adopting good norms from the people around us, we also learned not to be what some people were to us.

CHAPTER 20: EVERYTHING IS ILLUMINATED

KEY TAKEAWAYS

- Intense personal pains can deeply affect our souls to the extent of cracking it open. When this happens, we don't feel such pains alone, we become empathetic.

- When we have a blissful experience, things become clearer and it seems as if scales have just been removed from our eyes.

- Bliss is not being problem-free or perfect. Rather, bliss is a feeling that shows how we have grown wiser over the years making us to be present for the now.

- We can experience bliss by embracing every experience in life, good or bad.

SUMMARY

When one experiences bliss or some kind of euphoria, it is always difficult to express that experience in natural language. This is why when you speak of bliss you speak the language of metaphor because the very essence of bliss is itself, a metaphor.

Bliss is a transcendental, near-epiphanic experience that is immediately followed by a profound feeling of calm, contentment, gratitude, acceptance and joy.

Bliss does not really feel like reality, rather it feels like super-reality. It comes with an intense clarity and understanding of the connectedness of things. At the moment of bliss, earthly concerns and problems give way to a grander reality, a certain beauty mixed with awe that sparkles, as a new reality replaces the reality you thought you knew.

While some people experience bliss more often as they age, others are not so lucky. But that is because they have not looked. My dear sisters, if you look for bliss you will find it.

Bliss is everywhere. You can find bliss looking at the undulating waves at the beach; or the sun setting in the horizon as you sit on a bench in the park; or a nice plate of hot soup; or watching your grand child eat lasagna; or staring at your steaming cup of java (black, no sugar, no milk) in the thick of winter, or whatever. Bliss is everywhere.

But bliss does not always come from pleasurable experiences. Bliss can also come from pain. In fact, the fastest pathway to bliss is when one is ill and is told that they have a short time to live. That is when one sees with the most clarity how precious this life has been. Life cannot always be only good. In fact it is by embracing both the good and bad with the feeling of gratitude that we can experience bliss.

Whenever you experience bliss it is a good thing. But what we want is to experience bliss as often as possible. What better life can there be than one in which bliss is experienced continually?

It is my hope that my fellow women will continually experience bliss, one and all. And especially for us old women, may we continually experience bliss as we navigate through the currents of this last stretch of the river of life.

Let us embrace everything that comes to us. Let us embrace all of life, the joys, the pains, the disappointments, the rewards, the small moments and the grand occasions. It is through this holistic, this total embrace that we can reach the bliss that will carry us gently through this stage in our lives.

Dear sisters, my wish is of more bliss to you, one and all.

Cheers!

NOTES

NOTES

NOTES

NOTES

NOTES

NOTES

NOTES

NOTES

Summary of Atomic Habits by James Clear: An Easy & Proven Way to Build Good Habits & Break Bad Ones By BookNation Publishing

Summary Can't Hurt Me by David Goggins: Master Your Mind and Defy the Odds By Bob "Sarge" Kessone

Summary of BEST SELF by Mike Bayer: Be You, Only Better By BookNation Publishing

Summary of THE GREENPRINT by Marco Borges: Plant-Based Diet, Best Body, Better World
By BookNation Publishing

Summary of The Life-Changing Magic of Tidying Up: The Japanese Art of Decluttering and Organizing: A Guide to the Book by Marie Kondo
By BookNation Publishing

Summary of UNDER PRESSURE by Lisa Damour Ph.D.: Confronting the Epidemic of Stress and Anxiety in Girls
By BookNation Publishing